Dear Angel,

Moments of Metamorphosis

Thank you so much for
the support ✿

Wishing you all the
blessings !

Aaliyah

aaliyah arshad

To my loved ones, thank you for your constant advice, your encouragement and your unwavering support.

Thank you to genmi for the beautiful cover.

Contents

Introduction To My Galaxy

A Train to Nowhere

The moon is guiding me as I float by. I thank her for unveiling the way.

The hills glide by, sifting through the sky. Like petals sprouting, they open up to new ideas and lands. Clouds float above me, slowly cascading over the stars.

In this space, there is an untold story of the galaxy's shifting power. Constellations that map out parallel universes.

I have manifested tales of stolen ages, of corrupted cities and lost souls. I have seen men fighting turbulent wars and women crying for moments already passed. In this place lovers have laid down their weapons and swam together in harmonious melodies.

There is a sprinkling of words here that blossom into a garden of turquoise butterflies and lavender haze. A space where waves crash and swarm over feelings of broken glass and soft cotton. Somewhere in this moment, we lay our heads to rest, whilst we sink into a feeling of peaceful acceptance,

Leaning into our breath,

Evolving into our desired reality,

Becoming a new story,

Let me guide you through this celestial journey,

Let me swim into your soul so you can find your own moments of metamorphosis.

Part I. Universe

It's not that I'm invisible

It's that I'm above

I have a spirit that transcends

There is so much freedom here

I can feel the electricity in the clouds

Is that how thunder reigns down

Discovering myself is never more authentic

Writing about nature feels ingenious

I'm pawing at elements trying to sniff out balance

There's a way I move, flares wrapped up in idiocracy

Synchronised insanity

It's the kind of feeling you can't put into words

Love takes on new meaning

There is something that's festered here for so long

I can't understand the meaning behind old songs

Everything rhymes different, concealed from the person I once was

Running towards the sun

The poetry inside of me swims for the shore

Lapping along with the waves

I float seamlessly, echoing aimlessly

There's so much love to uncover

So much wonder to discover

Minds that don't match mine but they open my eyes

I was wrapped in a prison

Bars on my heart, I needed to expel my throat chakra

Tap into the third knowing, the state that exists and is flowing

Up from my root chakra you swam

Transcending into my bones and skin

There was a familiarity in this laughter

Scenes I had once repeated

There was no meaning other than the fact that your eyes shined like mine.

Interactions with a Stranger

I saw him sitting on that park bench again today. I went over and asked what was wrong. He replied, saying "why should anything be wrong?"

I saw that sad look in his eyes and wondered who he was pretending to be okay for. He was a different kind of stranger. The kind you look at twice when in passing. The kind you want to get to know. I wondered if he knew what others thought when they looked at him.

He continued to stare off into the distance. I didn't ask for his name. And he didn't ask for mine. We stayed like that for a while.

Then I walked away. I returned to my life and he returned to his.

Tell Me Your Symptoms

"Footsteps in the dark

Crying, their hearts breaking

Pulses I can feel just beneath my wrist

Heart is twisting, I can feel it squeeze

Stomachs that continue to twirl a perfect ballerina sequence

Eyes peering deep into my soul

Losing my balance

Twisting and spiralling, deadlines crawl out

Reminders that I too need to hurry

With so much to do

'We need to talk'

All the books I haven't read

Everywhere I haven't touched

People I have yet to meet

Falling for you when you can't see me

Or possibly losing my chance when you handed it to me

A fig tree with endless possibilities

A Sylvia Plath ending

Or worse no ending at all

Pollution poison perfectionism

Disaster death loss

Unhappiness failure

Loneliness."

"Please stop!"

"Shall I continue?"

My Friends and I

Can I ask you a question?

If this is too soon

If you don't have the answers

Don't tempt me with a message

And make me start to wonder.

Why did you fool around with us?

Distort my mind and

Make me a child to the plague inside my heart

Corrupt my friends' lives

Make them suffer at the hands of their distrust

Pollute our blood with lies

Of hope and something to hold onto

When really we continue to stumble in the dark

Grasping for something new

Blind because we've been taught that happiness is our end goal

We've been disfigured by this thing you call life

Beaten down and told to remain strong in times of strife

I no longer know what strength means

We are falling into pits of black that

Stay outside of our reach.

A Million Light-Years Away

A lonesome girl wanders silently on a distant star

Looking at the green and blue swirls smoking up her vision

Of a planet far away

Sprinkles of dust flitter around her

As she floats aimlessly away

Glitter swirling around her essence

The only company she keeps

Artificial gravity sinking her heart

So only deafening silence can be heard

Engulfing her senses

Filling up the bits of atom that disguise her as art

A lonesome girl wanders lost

Forgotten amongst the twinkling stars.

Loss of Youth

disillusioned at their best work it's not easy figuring out who you are, do you know what they mean when they ask those

fucked up questions of parenthesis and commas because they struggle to find another way

to ask if you know what you are supposed to be doing, it's not easy at the best of times

in those cobbled street corners and cracked pavements

the green weeds poking at the sides

to figure out who you are and what you're writing

looking at e.e. cummings or keats and wondering where they thought they could get off

writing things you don't understand

but the next generation of clueless idiots fuck up more than you in alleyways smoking the good stuff

wishing for the future because now isn't any good

oh but wait, fast forward and they're in the same place but they're all alone

wishing for the past because now isn't any good

"I saw the best minds of my generation" closed off and forced to work long hours with little pay

because their rent was calling

and it's all well and good having goals but dreaming won't pay the bill,

and who asks if you are okay when the words flow out of your mouth and the water spills out of your sides, those people

who fill the young generation with a loss of hope

who charge their energy into rectangular paper that won't make them happy but will sure make them full who run along the middle of the blazen roads of life, hot red coal tearing at your lungs

filling up the smooth eloquent marble of that posh hotel along Russell Square pretending you are something that you are not

so when they ask me who I am

I don't know what to say

because I'm busy focusing on trying to make the best of what I've got

I don't have time for your silly little games.

Four Seasons

Like a slight shuffle in the breeze

I feel my life take meaning

I inhale the whooshing of the wind

And ask the questions of every season.

See winter comes up large and billows its frost like icicles

Then spring settles in and transforms the chill into soft pink petals

Summer swims in like a wave cleansing the warm gold dust of its sins

Then autumn spirals over the sun and the crisp air settles in

And with every change I feel

The cycle of each breeze forms a shield

Refusing to bend or break

The earth takes hold of its power, stomps out our will with every breath
we take

So I ask this question with resolve

Do we know how to take care of a power that's out of our control?

Are we thoughtful enough to succumb to its will

And stop resisting the cycle it has to fulfil?

The Earth is Dying

1.

In the meadow she walks

flowers all around

daisies and daffodils

falling to the ground.

2.

In the meadow she walks

but the leaves have fallen down

something is stinging

the fumes are what surrounds.

3.

In the meadow she walks

and the dirt is on the ground

her feet and tears are swollen

her lungs are turning brown.

4.

In the meadow she walks

she's been beaten down

the plants have been crying

the earth is turning brown.

Secret Garden of the Soul

The flowers you grow in the garden of your heart
have become dehydrated, neglected for years
and it is a shame that they suffer because of your wrath,
because of your own self-loathing tears.
Growing from within you, stretching far and wide
the roots take shape and begin to grow
into the sunflowers and daffodils that you reject,
the beauty you deny is beginning to show.
You can pretend not to see the roses on your cheeks,
or the smile as bright as a buttercup
the pollen so strong it engulfs everyone
the charm of your elegance enveloped.
Your soul is an embodiment of tulips in summer
or daisies dancing with the wind
in an effort to flow with the yellows and reds
what tragedy you can't see your spring.

Comparison is an art form

A black canvas stands tall and proud,
  Slowly the colours of the galaxy swirl onto the blank space
    Like a wave ripples onto the sand
      Leaving its mark.
        Eventually the swirls form pictures
          Of elements and matter
            Leaving behind a mark of something
              lovelier
                something prettier
                something better.
                  Now the canvas is tainted with
                  The colours of the world,
                    The blue tears and green moss
                      Masking what's underneath because
                        Comparison is an art form
                        Where we become submerged.
                          Yet this canvas learns to shrink and stutter,
                          No longer tall and proud
                            The painting becomes what matters
                            And not the soul inside,
                              You see the canvas only views
                              The ones who observe
                              And it never sees itself
                                The patterns and the swirls
                                The beauty in and out.
                                  Because the focus is elsewhere
                                  On whom it's sure is better,
                                    Learning slowly that
                                      Comparison will kill you,
                                        It's life's longest oppressor.

Interactions with a Stranger Part II

I stood waiting at the bus stop.

A girl sat beside me. Her headphones in and her music loud, I think she was trying to block out the world. When she turned her head I saw a vacant look in her eyes. I began to wonder what her story was. I think she was struggling. But aren't we all?

Her struggle will accumulate to nothing. Soon she will be under the ground among the moss and mud and worms. Yet she is still trying. I wonder what that is. Why humans try so hard even though it doesn't matter in the end. The endless struggle. The endless cycle of self-hatred and worry. If I looked hard enough I began to realise she was less vacant and more sad. But she seemed good at putting up a front. She looked at me then and smiled. I was shocked so I forgot to smile back. I was shocked because despite everything, she still remembered to smile. I suppose that's why we continue to survive and evolve. Because we remember to smile.

A Different Colour

Are you scared?

When you see my chocolate skin do your bones make shivers within?

When my sister stops

With a cover on her head the same as the cover on your skin.

You see I'm scared

When my brother walks outside

And I don't know if he'll be here tonight

When my sister walks down that road

In the dark and no one knows

Because really who knows?

They only see mud where her soul is a bright silver ebony

Of love and happiness and philosophy.

You see I'd much rather hear about

A happy news where people live in harmony

But all I hear is more killings because of police brutality

And racist insanity

And people thinking that Muslim on that plane reading their dua is a threat to their humanity.

Oh Allah, Oh God, Oh Buddha,

Where has their love gone?

Oh Athiests, Oh Agnostics,

Why does no one sing our song?

You see I feel uncomfortable in my own skin

When I'm around people who think they're a better fit

In society,

They picture prosperity

While we picture more deaths more hurt more hunger more disparity.

I am beginning to think the talk is useless, what's the point of fighting when our voices get silenced...

But no,

Stop.

Don't give up your voice.

Your words are the stars that soar into a universe of matter that can change even the hardest disbeliever

Who disbelieves that change is possible, that the fight is never ending

Because one day we'll make it and our stories will be heard,

And the voices of the silenced

Will never be

Forgotten.

When the voices who've been martyred

Remain in

History's charter.

The art of self-hate

She was born to hate

the lines etched on her face

and she looks around and sees

all the beauty and all the popularity.

She wonders why they say

that she has a beautiful face

when she can clearly see

the reflections of her misery.

She watches the other girls

all of them, the essence of a pearl

a thing of magnificence

amongst a place of depressed deliverance.

She wonders why she can't

learn to love her ever-growing plants

the natural beauty of the others

she fails to see it, all she does is whither.

It's a tragic thing she knows

to repress and stunt her growth

just because she really can't see

anything about her that represents beauty.

And whilst she understands

that maybe one day she'll learn

how to love her flowers

for now the shame makes her cower.

Yes, I'm Loud

You ask me why my voice is so loud

When every time I scream I can't be heard above your pride

You shut me down with venom and then say my feminine energy is my vice.

I feel the need to be a foot taller than the crowd

Because it's only this tall that I break the ceiling you've trapped me in

And when I turn and look to my sisters

Their voices have gone hoarse

They've already tried to be distinct

And yes, my words are laced with fire

Because if I'm angry maybe you'll understand that this is dire,

We're suffering because we're told we belong on the ground

Make sure we don't stand out

Inviting snakes to slither in when we start to shout

But we didn't open our mouths just to let it be filled with spite

Men thinking they can cut us down

I'm looking at my sisters now and I feel tired

How do I make you take me seriously when you can't understand

What it's like to be the only one who feels like we need to fight?

Please

      don't silence me.

I am not something you can call weak

You mistake this burning prophecy as me burning down your house

I'm just making room for us to be the ones in charge

Become a soft wonderland that can also be hard

Be someone who can be made both of thorns and petals

Discard our shame and make it into soft nettles

18

A dichotomy of fight and flight

So yes, I'm loud

Because that is what makes me soft

I won't apologise for being more than you thought

My voice is both my weapon and my friend

And I am proud of what it means to be a woman.

Not Brown Enough

Am I too brown for you

Does my skin force you to face an uncomfortable truth

Do you run behind your mother and cower and cry

Because I embrace this melanin and refuse to hide

Is my pride something that makes you roll your eyes

Because I talk too much about the chocolate river running down my skin

And I strive to reclaim something my ancestors thought was a sin

Is everything according to you too much of a race issue

Should I pretend my culture isn't an important heirloom

Would it make you comfortable to sit behind screens

And watch reflections of you and not reflections of me?

Well what a shame the ocean of heritage within me that runs deep

Looks at you and doesn't blink twice at what it sees.

Disillusionment Creates Revolt

it was the best of times, it was the worst of times

but oh it was the worst of times

to see the faded dreams of the youth torn up and scattered amongst the tarmac pavement of their dreams,

being told who they are and who they cannot be because they weren't the ideal and they didn't live a life

of tea-time at five because that was when their shift started at their local shop. They wouldn't admit they knew

dickens, who doesn't know what to say himself

when the children are on street corners of their adolescence

selling yellow paper and faded dreams

broken down into distorted parts like petals on a flower

'does he love me, does she not?'

the most important questions for their youth,

what irony, oh sweet irony

when they're blamed for the very thing they tried to prevent

it's a corrupted generation of lies where no-one really tries

because what's the point of trying

when really all you're doing is slowly dying?

A System of Suffering

My identity was wrought with tragedy

Decided for me before I knew how to speak

I stumbled over paragraphs and numbers that made me weak

And then I crawled out of a system that expected me to succeed

But it cut me down, crushed my branches, destroyed my leaves

Assumed I could get by without water to feed me

Told me to spiral up to the sky without giving me the ability

Made green paper from my body and placed more importance on it than
my own mobility.

Now you stare at me and stomp until you hear my roots crunch

Sigh out in despair because you see me as the liar

Even though your system loves to mould me with a kick and a punch

You ask me why I can't seem to ascend any higher

But you profit off my suffering as you sit in your tower

And put me down for struggling to fight back against your power.

My tears become oceans that stream under me until I'm finally fed water

But even then my own self growth is stunted by my mind convincing me
I'm a failure

How can I grow tall when my tears are made of salt

The taste of me sprouting is fake and I'm suffering alone

I lower myself in shame and I block out any sun

And as I'm shrouded in darkness I drink every drop of doubt up.

Now my identity is wrought with tragedy

As I sink into the earth and lose the feeling of the sun's touch

I'm a self-fulfilling prophecy

A person designed by a system that is destined to rot.

My City

It's my city

I said that clearly,

I think they heard me

I'm not quite sure what I mean

Though...

Surely if this is my city

I'd feel comfortable

Wouldn't be intimidated to walk down my own road

Wouldn't be shy of my heritage

Wouldn't be scared to show people what I love

Wouldn't run from this narrative.

You see our parents are from here

This is all we know

You tell me I'm an immigrant

But my ancestry descends a few generations

My history is in my London city bones.

"Slyly I think they're trying me,

I work just as hard as him

Yet I'm still struggling.

Why can he afford the treatment I lack

That vegan health snack,

His government giving him his money back."

I know it's strange

Gentrification is a part of this town's name

You're only used to six pound sandwiches

Our communities are used to taxes and benefits,

We live on the same road

But I don't see you understanding me

You don't take time to listen

Pay attention to your privilege.

"It's just an area, why are you stressing?"

You don't know what it's like to face animosity

In your own home

Struggle against hypocrisy

Forced to conceal the need to explode,

It's my city,

But as I say it my voice falters

Maybe I don't belong here,

I'm told I need to disappear

Go back to where I came from

It's strange to hear those words

From a stranger who's just

Settled in.

What Do You Do For a Living?

I want this to be the thing I do,

When you ask me what I am I want to tell you this is my truth

That words flow from my brain for a living,

That the letters I write actually have meaning

I suffer the same as everyone,

Looking for a purpose in a universe of dust

Wondering if my words will ever be enough

Wondering if anyone will ever really listen

Looking for the thing that makes me want to keep living

I know you feel this too

I know that's why you write the same words I do

You may say it in different ways but you're still stuck in this tiresome game

Trying to find something to take home to your lover

To put food and rent on a silver platter and say it came from your own wonder

That someone actually listened to those words you wrote on a scrap piece of paper

Sat up and said I feel you, I can hear you, your passion deep under

Just know

I listen

Everyday.

I want this to be the thing we do.

Hollywood Hall of Fame

Welcome to the land of fame

Gold trees and green leaves pave the way

There's a twinkle in your eye

You're here to make your mark

You're coming in like a surprise.

They reach out a hand and help you up

Tell you to smile when the cameras are on

Then they pull you aside when it turns off.

They whisper and sneer until you don't know what's real

You block out your reality so the money can still heal

When you're alone and remembering how you got here

And they can use cloth made of sandpaper to dry your tears.

You see, they said it was easy

To get what you want

Just lie there and take it

Don't protest or say stop.

They sew zips onto the mouths of the ones who can help you

Buttons for eyes on the ones who know the truth

Seep into a system made of paper

Swim in corruption while you hold onto later,

When the money is pouring in

And you can turn and leave

And you forget why you even came,

There was no happy next to their greed

They just took what they wanted,

Forced you to be pleased

That they'd given you a leg up

When all you wanted was to get off of your knees.

Now I stand and watch you cry

You've gotten good at masking what's inside

They've told me all you do is lie

I'm not sure which story is right.

Do I trust this sinking feeling that distinguishes the light

Conceals your Cheshire smile deep into the night

So I can't see clearly and you've lost your sight?

  We're beginning to forget why this is our fight.

The Oldest Job In The Book

My body is not a commodity
But you sold me as property
Got rich off my assets
Didn't ask for my consent.
Then I took back the narrative, told them to treat me
As something more than an animal
To be devoured and touched like I'm nothing but a criminal.
This narrative has been written before the turn of the century
The oldest story in the book
Of learning how to be appealing
Because it's only my body that you're seeing,
I chose this for myself
For reasons that shouldn't matter
Whether this was for strife or pleasure,
I deserve better
Than an iron hand holding my throat
Telling me my only choice is to smile or choke,
Cough up words that you can't hear
You're too busy building barricades
Rules that keep me trapped by fear,
It's not for you to tell me whether I have the right to live.
You might think this is a sin,
But my beautiful vessel isn't something you can pin-

                                  point, tell me I'm a foil
of false identity, not worth the soil
I stand on, I'm tired of fighting for scraps
I demand to be more than your spoils.
I chose this life to keep me above water
Stop me from drowning under all the others.
I continue to fight with your stained sword
One day I'll be recognised as more than you are worth.

Is This Gentrification?

Some things continue to remain

Even when they have purged us out

When our souls no longer make a place in this space

The lights shine fluorescent under a twinkling star sky

But if you look closer you can see the lie

There is a bulb where the moon should be

The buildings reach higher than any spirit could take you

No God can stomach this truth

I think about what my God wanted

A place of serenity, a place to be free

And yet these false prophets took the land and made it an atrocity

There is no love in these pavements made of gold

Just people sleeping on cold cobblestones

We live a false identity

One that is moulded by greed, we fail to see our reality.

     I think we are beings of contradiction,

       Relying on the artificial light but searching for something else.

The moon is shining behind the clouds

It lights up the sky in waves and different sounds

It penetrates the false lies

And the unnatural visions up high

So that despite the destruction of the land there is a reason to smile

And even if we survive

A dichotomy will continue to rise between the day and the night

The black stains and the pure plight

We hope for a world where substance matters over style.

 I'm not sure when that time will arrive

 I pray for a time when we can stand hand in hand together.

I watch my city crumble to make way for grey, black and white

But I will not stop trying to pour colour into everyone's sight

I see the ones who understand that this is a never-ending fight

A struggle that will continue to make its way into us

Until we can no longer see the truth

We can't distinguish between the ones we love and the ones who want

To hurt us, keep us suffering

So we rely on them and then they're all we see

Their buildings are the only ones we need

If we live by their rules surely we'll still be seen

Taken care of when we can no longer be.

I still can't climb the road that leads to a better place

I find myself besides the ones who suffer alone in a world of greed

The ones staring into the empty apartments with false light

And the moon is still burning bright

Besides the repetition and the lucky ones who live out of sight

I remember a past where all we could see was the moon shining down on
blades of grass

Now I sit in a city wondering why they fashioned everything out of glass

Why there is poison next to pieces of art

Maybe I wander alone

I forgot that this town is no longer mine to call home.

Employment Benefit Creates Deficit

He's a walking grave

Laying a path that will only result in him withering away

They grind him down, force him to work when he can't

And he has no one to turn to

The only ones who reach out a hand live his same truth

Forced into boxes because of misinformation in their youth

Or life sending them down a path they didn't choose

Because it's easier to live if you have a job

But is it living if your labour is your only worth

Why do we only care what they can provide

And ignore them when their lives become a suffering strife

You see he is a story like so many others

Told you're not fit to work

But you can't get no benefits

Don't scrounge on the council

You don't get to reap the benefit

Of all the hard work you put in year after year

You got to this place and hard work doesn't matter here

They only care about numbers and fulfilling a quota

While you sit at the job centre wishing someone would lend a shoulder

And they tell you to suck it up

Be a soldier

But what's the point of fighting if all it does is make your life violent

So he gets to a point

Where he's no longer living

Vulnerable to a system

That will always be unforgiving.

Starvation of Hope

I lost hope years ago

Sat on the brink of despair watching the ones I love choke

Intoxicating fumes filling them up

Struggling to make ends meet, they would start but never stop.

We would sit there everyday

Watch you from your ivory tower

Even when we begged you for any last scrap you saved

You would look down on us, cringe and cower.

And what's so wrong with wanting to survive

You store your greed in a trophy and put it on show with pride

But whenever we asked for help

You'd shout at us like we're the reason we live in this hell.

Our children are sitting here sweating out our last pay

You see they've learnt to stop asking questions

Stay silent because it's easier that way

They get tired but they've learnt their lesson

Every look they give us is shrouded in dismay

And you stand there with a heel on their throat

You'd rather let them starve than watch them hope

Gold and green rivers run throughout your castle

But all you'll give them is grey slush to keep them full

I'm growing tired of complaining

It's easier to submit to your will

I'll stop talking if you'll let them start winning

I can't bear to see them look at us with any more guilt.

Just Another Statistic

Maybe if I was quieter

My voice would be permissible

Maybe if I was submissive

You'd lose reasons to make my life amendable

I'd suffer and you'd cry

Because my skin was a shade you recognised

Statistics wouldn't be interchangeable with lives

And our voices would flow, not cut like knives

But you blindfold your eyes when you look at us

You hold a gun and ensure the safety's not on

You smile when our soul slips away

Because you're the hero who saved the day

You turn around and say you've paved the way

For yet another to lap up every word you say

I learn to be submissive

But even that won't save my spirit

As long as my skin retains a threat

Your hands will be pressed against my neck.

Up in Flames

Up in flames you came

tearing through blazing roads and crumbling walls

poisoning blood and polluting minds

indoctrinating innocents with corrupted lies.

You ask me why there can't be peace

when 10,000 of us have died

and even then I do not know where my sister went last night

she has not returned and you do not care

you continue to terrorise us, you point and stare.

I am a passer-by in my own town

you have swept shame into every life

blushing, cringing, skin crawling with pitiful cries

of desolation and destruction and demolition.

'Quick, quick, you must escape' we hear them say

as you storm into what was once a castle and make it a cheap façade

of peace and coalition, you encompass every child's vision

to be something more than the rubble at their feet.

Now here we are, so many years later

and the generations continue to live in slander

they do not know what this peace is you talk of

for all they can see is the destruction you have wrought

so when you ask me why we can't live in peace

please ask yourself where your footsteps have been.

Borders

My soul has swam across oceans

Through turbulent waves rocking me back and forth

Holding onto dust slipping through my fingers

Only to be told I don't belong.

My tears have travelled through generations

Down streams of icy water piercing my skin

Protecting the ones I love through false promises

Only to be told I'm better off sinking.

The broken land we left behind

Becomes the dust that stings our senses cold

As we drift away from the home where we thrived

Only to be told we're a poison, that they need to take back control

But where was our control when our sacred temple turned to rubble

At the hands of the ones who want to leave us on our own

When all we want is a place where we can seek solace

Yet you choose to build borders made of stone.

So find our souls on these rocky shores

Lost and ripped apart from the only ones who we ever loved

Our hearts are broken into pieces we use to build shelter

Because protection is a privilege we will never know.

An Unfamiliar Home

I know I've said this all before

Words like lyrics flowing onto paper transforming my thoughts

I know this was happening long before I was born

But this is blackening my very own soul,

You see I spoke in words and voices that weren't always my own

Trying to relay a message of golden pavement turned to stone

Spoke from perspectives I wanted to get across

To the rich and powerful who refuse to let anyone discuss,

But this time these letters spilling out of my mouth

Come from a heart that's been crushed

Because the pavement I walked on when I was a child

Has been trod on and spat on and turned into rust,

The buildings are shiny and glisten with false hope

They look like diamonds but stand closer you'll see

They're knives itching and begging to cut our throats

They glimmer and pierce us with their burning prophecies,

They say now that the streets are shiny and new

Everything is better and everyone can bloom

Yet when I look around and search for my friends

I see their homes crumbling and all that's left is their gloom,

Everything I knew that was familiar and beautiful

Has been destroyed so green paper can pave a new way

The home where I made my first memories with you

Has become a lost paradise that is beginning to eternally fade,

The colours and hues of purple and pink

Are replaced with cool tones of black and grey

Because that's what those towering giants drink

Profit disguised as trends because that is what pays,

This poison they spilled that's spreading so quickly

Moves me to words that flow like a water droplet on a vast sea

Hope becomes something we fail to grab hold of

Gentrification becomes a part of our identity.

Home Is Where The Heart Is

I'm looking for my roots

But I don't where I'm rooted

A colony shines brighter

When it has no resistance

I don't know about my heritage

That's a conversation we avoided

Because trauma is collective

And memories don't let you go so easily

You get ripped apart and lose your identity

Travel across seas to be told you're a walking felony

No wonder you don't want to speak to me

It's hard to learn about my history when it's wrapped up in your tragedy

I suffer from a loss of land

But I don't know where that land is

Born and raised in a home where I don't recognise my family

I can tell you she's called ammiji

But I don't know her story

What a shame I seek something out of reach

It's a joke because I can't even speak

Tried to communicate with my ancestors when I was young

Lost it when I grew older, fell out of touch

I write more about Palestine than Pakistan

Not saying one's more important than the other but one holds my past

Ek minute beta, I keep studying to make this memory last

I know partition from the books

I know horror exists in my blood but I don't want to look

You tell me they travelled all that way by foot

Looking for independence

Now I've become dependent

Every day I get older my friends ask me questions

I don't have the answers and I'm not sure you want to think about the consequence

We make a home wherever we can

Sniff out the best spot to call our own land

And still we struggle to belong to one man

We're rooted in history but we don't know where we stand.

Nationality and Borders

When I cut myself open I bleed red not blue

But that's funny because so do you.

What will it take for me to prove that we're the same?

That just because my ancestry swims across generations and different oceans

Doesn't mean we don't hold the same pain

And aren't you the one who put me here

You were an immigrant in my land first

Telling my father's father that his only purpose is to serve

Bend over to your will

Submit his labour so you can excel

Flash forward and we made a living off the bones you propelled

Built houses and roads because that's all you would allow

Then we sent our children to live by your rules

Was it assimilating or immigrating when they became your tools

And when one of our children defied your will

Suddenly we were no longer yours

You moulded our identity until we were made up of your flaws

Had to forget we were ever anything but British

Because if we show pride in our heritage all you'll do is strip us

Take away the one place we started to belong

Rip us from our loved ones until we're left alone

It's irony that the ones telling us we have no home

Are the ones who went searching for a place to call their own

All I can do is cut myself and bleed

Hope you see this not as violence but as an act of vulnerability.

A Dream Of One Man's Land

We were pushed out of our land before we could create something innovative

We brought ideas that poured creativity into their seas.

Nothing really mattered.

They didn't see our wisdom as truth,

Just curses in foreign tongues

They couldn't understand our dua was their manifestation

We had brought dreams alive through our beliefs and perseverance

Toiled across harsh terrain and broken cracks

Through an inferno blazing with the anger of oppression

We built a spot on a new land

Created prosperity through our own hands

Helped our ancestors walk tall and proud

Yet all they saw was our brown beauty

As a stain on their white sheet

A permanent mark they wanted to control but not to keep

They stole us from that soft place made up of sugarcane and sweet tea

Took us to a land where all we could see was depravity.

I want to go back there,

I don't belong there.

My ancestors don't recognise my foreign tongue

I whisper in their faith

Pray to Allah, bend down on my knees in the same way

But the snow-driven land takes up my space now.

And still I don't belong.

This piece of grass isn't mine

Doesn't hold the key to my past

Just a taster of the blood spilled and broken hearts.

There is a place we call home

A no-man's land where Bishan Singh took his last breath.

I still search for it even though it is oceans away,

I hold onto my past, I breathe, I pray.

In Response to Terrorism

There is a word in Arabic that means peace

And it is the word we use every day when we greet

Our mothers, our friends, our enemies.

Salaam my brother, you may not remember me

But I saw you on the TV

You said every side is equal and we should all be free

But our freedom is called into question

Until you paint us like we're the oppressors

Call our search for human rights a terrorist plight.

You see every day we stay on this land you lock us down with frowns and plans,

Plans to make our words into bombs

So that our call to prayer sounds like a threatening song

And all we do is advocate for peoples' lives

But you turn our search into a fight

Because it's easier to paint us as violent

So that we just stay silent when the ones who can help us deem us defiant

So Wa'ailakum Assalam brother

When I say hello I wish you peace

I pray one day you'll wish the same for me.

Western Imperialism

My hands are tied

I've been staring at the screen for too long

Wondering who was advocating for my side

You see they sit there in thrones made from our bones

And the funny ones give them attention because they teach them repentance

The ones with green eyes sinking into every crevice

Blackening each soul with letters

Are the ones who give these power hungry lions their substance

Something to portray a public pretence

Of caring about the ones who let them in

Our voices weren't heard and we learnt to submit

To the ones in the towers who controlled the power making us crumble and cower

To their reliance the need to live by their screens

To reach family and to see our future not our reality

And the word free market seems like we're free

But really puts us in boxes until we can no longer see,

Our information comes from warped ideologies

So the ones who give us a home leave us without a soul.

You cut me open and stood there while I bled

Then cursed when I turned your carpet red

Stained your tapestry until you kicked me out

Left me on the streets to fend for myself.

You walked past me when I begged for your help

Carved your knife into my skin

Made my body into a portrait of your sin

Then accused me of damning your beauty

I watched as you charmed them with your laugh

Wondering if they knew what you tore up

I crawled after you even as you drank me until the last drop

I guess I couldn't stop holding onto what once was.

A Tale of Plague

Who do I blame for making me this way?

I was blissfully ignorant of all the black stains

Then you came along and clawed your way

Into every screen, everything I see

You stand on a podium and block out our cries with your screams

Claim you're saving us when you're the ones who make us live in tragedy.

You see I watched my uncle die when he had so much to live for

One year away from watching his daughter blossom into something more

But you let disease come and swim its way into him

And then blamed all of us for the mess that you put us in.

You said the services we pay for needed our help

Made the frail army-serviced men walk around like a dog chasing its tail,

I watched loved ones around me break down and cry

While you see the darkness coming and you run and you hide,

But we're the ones who put you there standing on broken glass

And now we're the ones who pay for your life to continue to last.

I'm getting cynical with every year that goes by

Because every year another person I know continues to die,

Sometimes I catch myself angry at those around me,

Blame them because it's tangible and it's easy

But you're the one who convinced them you'd save their souls

And instead you plagued their minds like you were just burning coal

Trying to keep that fire going to help you stay warm

The people believed your words and they lived by your word

Now they're the ones suffering and I'm lost for words

I'm tired and I can't do this anymore.

Old News

I am telling myself to stop

Or maybe I'm telling you

I think I've lost my voice

It's coming out unclear what clarity is because clearly the reason I feel this way is because of you

Or is it the news?

Last night I heard them talking

Oh no, here we go:

"There's another Paki blocking up my radio

He's got a beard and a suspicious looking face

So don't tell me not to panic when he enters a new place

Aren't you afraid whenever you leave your house?

Allah knows I am.

Didn't you hear what happened in Paris, Manchester and Barcelona and now you want to let them in?

Soldiers are dying trying to fight for our right to be British

So don't tell me to be forgiving.

I mean, I do like me a bit of chicken teriyaki on a Sunday night

And don't get me wrong those red dress things look awfully nice

I appreciate the fact that Mohammad gave me a discount at my local shop

But we can't be lenient, we've got to tell them to stop

Stop sympathising with the terrorists if you wanna be one of us."

I think I'll turn the radio off now and listen to something else

But when I turn the channel I'm faced with the same old hell

Syria, Iraq, Palestine and far far away we've got children dying,

People like you trying to escape.

I guess it's different in those places because they're all used to this,

So I'll just turn off the radio and go back to pretending it doesn't exist.

Different But The Same

All we've ever known is to live in fear,

teach our children to prepare for war

everyone's scared of the unknown

kids are growing up learning to hate

learning about prejudice that irate

the ones who don't hesitate

to shoot someone who isn't the same

as their mother or sister or brother

but wait.

That's only a colour.

Your kid used the same paint

to draw a picture of someday

where the world is better

and the people live in harmony, together

so excuse me if I'm wrong

but am I not the same as you once were?

Do we not both look at the same sky

teaching each child they can fly?

The irony is tragic,

you hurt the only ones with logic,

and don't correct my manners

when we are made of the same matter.

A Women's Fight

My plight is formed from the blood of my ancestors

They struggle to sing the songs they wrote

Because their world was torn and they watched their buildings crumble

Now I stand here in their place with my own tarnished sword

The glass ceiling looks different from where we lie

Women before us tell me they paved the way

But I still have to climb steps that reach out too high

While those women complain about the new struggles they face

Still it's okay, we still sing the song together

Even though my work looks different to yours

Because despite the branding society stains my soul with

I rise higher and smash that ceiling with the power of our cause

And one day when I'm standing next to the sun

I'll reach my hand out and pull you up.

The scent of something new lingers on my lips

You ask me to define what this is

But how can I define a feeling I was convinced did not exist

You see when I was born I heard the moon whisper to the sun

Insisting acceptance was the only thing we could ever love

A nation born so different was never won

By convincing us we could only love a particular kind of someone.

Yet every blossoming petal sprouts anew

Because it cannot resist the sunrays helping it bloom

It learns how to love something new

Learns that natural is when it's lying next to you.

We have learned to love what we thought was forbidden

Discovered sunlight can overpower the moon

And we felt a connection to something that had been hidden

Found the golden light illuminating us was no longer taboo.

The Unwritten Story

How do I explain it

That pit in my stomach every time I walk at night

The feeling of dread when I meet their eye

It's not something I can show you

Tell you how it's not something in particular you do

But just you being you

Makes me sit on an empty carriage

Play out scenarios in my head

Of how I'll explain it to my family when you rip me to shreds

You might have a wife or daughter back home

But I won't know anything except the way your presence creeps into my bones

That fear is deeper than anything I've ever felt

Because it's knowing I'm a lamb inside my own shell

You couldn't relate, you don't see me as a threat

But panic sinks in when I'm isolated and alone

Stranded with just the threads of something that hasn't happened yet

Please don't blame me

I don't mean to assume I know you

But don't come near me

I don't have the energy to run away.

Ask Me Something

"Do you believe in love?"

"I believe in pain,

in the hurt inside every soul

the way a mother reaches out to her child

who is too distanced to notice.

I believe in searching,

I believe that you're yearning

for something

too far away.

What is love anyway?

Just a word to tear us apart inside

make us feel lonely when we can't cry.

It's broken up into slithers of need.

I don't know what I believe."

My Superpower

When I was young and forming my words

Teachers told me the skills I lacked

Framed my world around what I didn't deserve

Made sure my thinking was caged in a box

For so long I wondered about the threads tangled inside of me

Searched for a sense of who I was by comparison

Hoping the ones I looked up to would give me clarity

Only to find my soul resisting conformance

You see I was sewed together with a delicate hand

That knew I was born to stand out

Because the shape of my thoughts swimming about

Is unique and deserves to let its voice shout

Shout out to the ones who mistook my words

For submission when really I'm special

My process might be different from you

But my perspective shapes this world into something beautiful

Now I stand here with a stance of defiance

Proud of my golden hues amongst a sea of grey

My world shines brighter with my own guidance

And I'm learning to be new every day.

Do you realise that you've hurt us?

Maybe you forgot you were us

Living in an ivory tower

You thought you could do better.

What's better than the hurt you gave us

Telling us we're not worth it

We don't deserve the same benefits

The hand-outs you've been giving to yourself

Hurting all those at a disadvantage

You've taught us to hurt ourselves

Left us crying in disbelief

Holding onto your wealth

You'll say we caused our own grief

I don't know if the cause is worth dying for

What have we got left, who are we rooting for?

Even if I'm left with no hope

Even if you thought we were a joke

Do you realise you'll be left with no one

Sabotaged by your own gun

I know you only care about your own soul

I forget there's a devil in your own home

Maybe if you look in the mirror

Who you are will become clearer.

Are You Tired Yet?

I've started learning what it feels like to be tired

My energy's running out, I'm scared I will expire

Before I can do something to help inspire

Future generations not to take this poison and let it fester into fire

But I'm tired of using the word I

This isn't about me, it's not about my life

When we've got kids running scared selling food because they don't know any wiser

How are they supposed to help their mum when she's been told she can't be hired

Even though she's only here because the people barricading her are the ones who forced her to run and hide

Teach her kids that they can be anything but they need to accept they'll never be white

Never know what it's like to walk past that blue and white uniform and not fear for their lives

And it's a shame we can't tell them everything will be alright

That when they get older opportunities will begin to arise

Just stop scrounging on the rich because they didn't make you a cripple with a walking stick

Because opportunities only exist if you can afford to pay the price

What do we tell families living on benefits

That can't work because they're disabled but the government doesn't really give a shit

Maybe they just need a helping hand

And we've got to keep lending it

Making the steps easier to climb for every generation that wants to keep climbing it

Show them that yes it's hard to fight and it might get tiring

But we didn't get this far from holding back and not letting our words do the firing

Just show them that as long as we keep moving in a direction that stops the greedy from conspiring

Then at least maybe we have a chance to do something inspiring

That leads to a world that gives us a leg up when we decide to start climbing.

A Poet's Mind

I find solace in the written words of poets

They capture those 26 letters

And turn them into a new kind of power,

Enough to make a man cry tears of wonder

Or make a women stand up higher.

My love seeps into every teardrop that falls onto paper

As I descend into my own thoughts and lyrics

Hoping to transform the tightening in my chest

Into something more,

Something maybe you can read

And weep

Feel it in your own heart crawling deep.

Find comfort within my words please

You see these writers are just trying their best

They are just like you,

Trying so hard to find some kind of truth

What a beautiful thing it is

To spill your soul onto paper and leave the rest with your reader

What great trust you must have in humanity

To hope they see you as something deeper

I find solace in the written words of you.

I'm trying not to feel lately

Grew so tired of writing the same story

One of loss and heartache

One where I couldn't understand my own name

Looked at myself in the mirror and tried to transmute pain with more pain

But I've been charging my crystals lately

Looking at the sun and wishing for it to come

Every day I wake up and feel the heat and thank God for reigning down on me

I clutch onto sprinkles of dust like they're stars

Each one died before it could rest in my arms

But I'm thankful, grateful for the way I can see how quickly clouds move under the sky

Planets so distant, I'm glad

I'm a far-away fairy with magic on my hands

I created these words, even though they are simple letters

They acknowledge something greater

My hands are stained with paint because every day I depict something new

Flowers pink, purple and blue

Grass tickling underneath and lavender deep in my skin

I'm casting spells so that my reality can bend to my will

This is my quantum leap

There is a voice that rings deep.

A bell chiming incessantly.

Or maybe a knock.

Feel the beats pulsating beneath me.

I surge with new energy

Close my eyes and feel the adrenaline.

Something filling me up and it won't stop.

I feel insane but I am in love.

Look in my mystique mirror,

Who exists that shines brighter?

I burn the glowing sprinkles of firelight,

No celestial time for not generating

I say the truth, gazing at all of us.

We manifest our desired reality.

Feel the words sink into your cells and regenerate your mind.

Resurrect right now.

Let the earth breathe you in and out.

I am I.

Speech

the desire to get the words out bubble up in your throat

the letters are closing in on you

each word forming a sentence flowing through your mind like a wave
rippling the ocean,

swimming across your throat,

an intense sensation to let them spill out of the gaping hole in your face

so natural as speech should be.

You can feel the ocean inside of you burning up

and if you don't let go the words will set alight inside you

and then who knows what will happen?

So you must and you need and you desire

      to let the waves wash out your own dispelling thoughts.

Looking for Answers

I'm not sure where life is taking me

I'm lost in a sea of uncertainty

Everyone around me has found a beginning

Or they're searching for an end

Why are we so lonely?

I can't find an answer

I've been looking for so long

Waves have gripped my soul since my eyes fluttered open

A creature settles deep inside of me

A longing, a lump, a wall.

I do not know what I have found

Darkness continues to flitter over the night

Even the sprinkling of stars cannot filter the disappearance of light

And I am certain I will stay lost, stay gone.

I see the need for company,

Every time the sea grips the shore

It clings to it.

Every time we see a soul

We cling to it.

A Poem For My Ego

It's hard to be vulnerable

Hard to get words out on a page and make it make sense

You see I let my ego take over sometimes

I've learnt presence,

I've learnt self-acceptance,

Yet still this voice inside tells me I'm not enough

That the lyrics I spill don't resonate with love

And even in the moments where I become proud

Proud of the words flowing out my mouth

I look around and my eyes disguise each face as a frown

I'm convinced a lack of conviction makes me fall into the crowd

Because if I'm too vulnerable and you can't relate

All I'll do is sit back and slam myself, slowly deflate

Criticise my words when they actually mean something

Convince myself I should take the pen away and let my words become nothing

Now this piece has become a demon inside of me

I'm letting words flow out but I'm forgetting to breathe

It's my ego talking to you now

Placing expectations every time I'm in front of a crowd

Afraid to be, afraid to stand out

Scared if I do I'll get shut down

And even though this is a weakness I'll let it out

Because it's at my weakest that I can start to be proud.

     Actually,

If I'm being honest

It's the feeling of failure

Feeling an ocean in me but being unable to express it

Wondering if people relate or if they're just helping my essence

If honesty is a blessing

And these words are my only outlet

Then knowing I might be rejected

Makes me scared to believe

That this path is for me

It's the only place I'm connected, it's the most I've felt free

Yet still my ego stands tall and asks for silence

And every pen stroke I make is starting to feel violent.

Friends Forever

You ask me why I find it so hard to open up my heart

to have a little faith in people

and understanding when elements get mixed up

and life becomes hard

and people stop fake smiling to cover the mirror reflecting their broken shards.

Waves are crashing further away from me

and the tide won't come in,

I've learnt that trust is hard to earn

when the wound is self-inflicting

because those

       people

don't really care if you're struggling

they've got their own friction.

Stop trying to make it better, stop giving them what they want,

                         you're such a pushover...

They make you weaker,

an unbeliever

I'm not pretending to dislike you

I swear we had some laughs

but I'm finding it quite difficult

to look past your façade.

Who Do You Forgive?

I don't blame you for your poison

You are just like all the others

Polluting your surroundings.

How could you know

That you would infect my soul?

I'm trying not to blame you for your betrayal

You are the same tedious story

Trying to make me enticed

And disrupting my peaceful life.

But it's so hard not to blame you

When you sit there and smile

While you watch the glass shatter

And you chip away at my dark matter.

The Stars In-Between Us

Part of me wonders where you are,

What you are doing

So far away from us, up amongst the stars

You're too distant and your brightness is resisting

Everything that belongs on earth.

Part of me wonders who you are,

Why were you so lonely

Pondering a reason to stop your aching heart

Your happiness receding with a tragic unbelonging

Trapping you into the other.

Part of me wonders why you are,

When did you stop believing

Your essence a flickering light in the galaxy

Choosing to be the sun when you could shine with us

And now our connecting string snaps.

Nostalgia

These words that fill the page take up our soul

The ache of our hearts transformed from our core to the flowing sensation of our hands

I watch the words glide onto the paper like the way

leaves fall to the floor and I think of the way we all strive to be different

but our thoughts are all the same.

i miss what it was like back in the old days when we didn't have a care in the world with

the innocence and youth of laughter ringing in our ears

because we had no reason to let sea salt glide down our face.

And now we are changed

And our friends aren't the same

And our laughter stops

short.

Buzzing Together and Apart

Buzzing

Flowing through me coursing

Through my veins

The world is spinning like

The universe is insane.

The friends sit in a circle, eyes swimming into each other

Thinking their own thoughts of a world in their own specific matter

Atoms and particles and stardust in their souls

Flowing into the air around them and through their river,

A different buzz comes from their laugh as they stare at one another

And think of the world that they live in together.

She paints her voice onto a scrap of paper while her friend writes the veins of her own mind.

The wonders of their soul shatters, fallen together so we mix.

And at once we become each other, so together yet so far apart

Our own thoughts buzzing with a mixture of the love in our heart.

We are a product of our universe and as we sit here and produce our own matter,

We are aware of the matter we give each other

A new buzz,

And an old buzz.

On Top Of The World

And so we returned to the same place

Cold wind seeping through our bones

Same smiles on our face

That feeling we once had

Emotions running wild

All comes swimming back

Our souls are catching fire

Music is coursing through our mind

Our fingers are losing feeling

But it's funny because we're not shy

To remember every spark and fever.

Youth we once were

No longer the same characters

But each of us holds a piece

That we can fit back together.

You see, the fire won't stop burning

Until someone forgets the sticks

But as long as we don't forget

We can forever live like this.

Rocky Shores

Bumpy rides make for the greatest surprise

But you forgot to leave the safety belt on

I watched your regret spill out with great cries

As you left behind the soul you'd spent years working on

You told me how to sew patches on broken skin

Taught me how to pour water over words that hurt like sin

I'm watching you with painful reserve

Wondering where your essence has been

The aura oozing out of your skin has turned a muddy brown

I'm looking for you, watching you sink deeper

As you keep pushing your lyrics further down

Concealing words with a past that gleams brighter

But you're so lost I forgot that past doesn't exist

Wondering where your presence is

Finding your soul broken down into tiny distant pieces

I'll hold out a hand made of broken skin

Hope will help you grip it as tight as your heart closing in

Let these words flow through you like a river

Let it wash over all the words that hurt you more than sin.

A Shakespearean Tragedy

Isn't it ironic?

We spent the better part of our lives

Writing love letters with false words

And then we grew up and realised

Each page of the chapter we turned

Was broken down into discarded letters

Notes on a page that made no sense

Ideas that swam away from us

Until we couldn't find any words we actually meant

Because in reality you erased the letters we'd grown together

Watched them prosper only to fester jealousy towards their growth

Convinced yourself that if you set fire to the page you'd feel better

And forgot that I was the one that picked up a pen when you could no longer cope

I'm not sure this is irony

Most likely your story is one of tragedy

I'll write you into a blank verse

Move on from the memories

Successfully let go of all the hurt.

Don't treat me like a raindrop when I am the ocean

You see me as a ray of light when I am the sun

You perceive me like a cloud when I am the sky

Don't treat me like a fluorescent light when I am the stars.

I am a timeless goddess streaming along the waves of the universe

Who has more important things to accomplish than waiting for you

So do not take me for granted

And then ask why my existence is as fleeting as the universe you try so hard to connect with.

Soulmates Part II

There is a part of me that still believes

Soulmates are meant to be

Flying high together never losing wind

But I have watched you soar like Icarus

You've clipped your wings but you can't smell the smoke

And my heart still aches for you

Because it's blinded the elements of truth

You mistake the night sky for ominous light

I want to scream and help you see the stars beneath your cries

But I can't help you and I've learnt not to hold onto something that cannot be renewed

I have learnt time and again that the ones who need time

Will find it even if it means they're not by your side

And I have convinced myself that this is not the end

That we will meet again

If not this life then the next

When our souls see each other they will not say nice to meet you but good to see you once again

And even if you never see my face

You'll carry me all the way

Into the old age that comes too quickly

Before we know it we're not the same

Our hearts are changed

I will learn to be okay with whatever is thrown my way

I will not cling to you if it stops you swinging

Through the trees

And this might be the last time these words find their space onto this page

But it won't be the last time thoughts of you remain.

73

Growth

I'm trying to get better

At turning my feelings into a letter

Rather than letting it fester into something that leaves me bitter

I've got better at acceptance

But I'm still grinding my way through this mess

Trying to make sense of emotions I'm constantly left with

It's not a perfect world

Where I sit and ponder at the blackening sky

Looking at stars,

Wondering why I made myself feel like an insignificant dot in other people's eyes

It's a tired old fable

Like a record left spinning, a headache on the turntable

I keep repeating myself

Because I'm convinced if I make the wrong move they'll desert me and I'll be left unstable

So I've been trying to purge out my ego

Let it simmer away until it can't prosper

Convince me I'm something that should be left to suffer

It's a difficult world

But it gets easier as I sit and ponder

Look up at the blackening sky with its twinkling stars

Learning I can be kind to myself and also kind to others

That the ones I love know my true intentions

And make time to love myself for being a soldier.

Growing Up

Puberty is something that happens only once in your life

Heartbreak when she says she doesn't want to be around you

Cruel words that affect who you are

I am aware when they say age is just a number

That is their way of trying to wake me from my slumber.

I wanted to feel 19 when I was 16

Then turned 22 and craved disparaged youth

Now I'm walking on twisted vines

Trying to find a clear path

Hoping one will shine out in the dark

I don't feel so young anymore

The cells on my body regenerate faster than I can keep track

I want to call out to time

Ask it to walk slower

My footsteps can only make small marks

But its arrogant laugh rings out in this twisted forest

Its strides get longer and soon I am running to keep up

Out of breath I wheeze with the trees

With every passing exhale they're dying a little quicker

Suddenly death is creeping up on me

I reach out and give it a hug.

Puberty is something that only happens once

I am walking slower

The earth is putting me in a trance.

Testimony To Our Youth

Today was something new

I held your hand as we stood on the precipice

Too scared to jump in

But we thought we could take it

We were younger than our years

Even now I feel it

The youth spills off of me and runs down my sides

Standing here amongst the faces I've memorised

Their lines etched in my mind

It's filled with love

Your heart swells when we look at them

Maybe for the first time we belong

You see I've found emeralds in rocks

Crystals shine in the places we forgot

I'll hold them close to my heart

Watch you stand there with the moonlight reflecting off the river

And I'll hold onto each word you let shimmer

Your thoughts swirl into me

I feel together we're complete

And we stand here now

Filling in the gaps of the stories we tell

Learning we're happy being this way forever

I'm understanding that this is the universe setting out a plan

And I'll go along with anything you said

Let's shine together as we stand on the edge.

The Passing of a Soul

My tears are washing into the ocean

And I'm mistaking them for rain

I don't know if I'm crying for the fragility of you

Or the certainty of pain.

My hands remain unsteady

As my pen wavers on words unsaid

Because whispers hurt like fractures

When I whisper the words of the dead.

A soul begins slipping away

I close my fists, grip hold of time

I should learn not to be afraid

Should learn to accept what's mine.

Eternity, turn my ego into shatters

Envelop my senses

Consume stars back into matter

Break down my last defences.

An Ocean Wave

It started as an ocean wave

Reaching out to the grainy sand trying to shelter it from the pain

Protecting it at all costs, no shame

Hoping it would get used to the rain.

But the ocean couldn't stay,

It tried its hardest but the tide refused to listen

Pulling those waves back to regain its strength

So it could become an entire ocean that glistens.

Eventually this new wide ocean learnt what it meant to exist

To realise its worth and not strain itself to be something it could not manifest

Something it did not know how to balance and risk a loss of its power

Learning that the sand can exist without the oceans constant showers

That rain is satisfying and can help it grow

That the ocean needs to claim the waves as its own.

And now watch the ocean flourish

Huge and wide and nourished

Learning that love is learning to be patient

Learning that it's okay to be selfish.

Old Journals

Faded pages flicker open

The curtains spreads out amongst the wind

Reminding me of what could have been

Yellow stains on the memories of the people we loved

Letters telling stories we held together when we were young

Dreaming of a youth made up of love

Now I sit here turning each page alone

Looking at old stories we told

Of days when we couldn't imagine a different future

Never thinking that solitude equals growth.

The Trees Whisper Secrets

Once again she sat there

Solitary on a park bench wondering who was left

Whose souls still drifted next to hers

The trees whispered in the breeze

They seemed to answer her question with indignation

Cynical once again

You should discover yourself

And time again she does

Learns what the breeze is saying

How the water moves with time

Learning to flow and not hold onto something lost

The trees are louder now

They say it's okay

To be alone and tall

Proud and small

That's what makes a genuine soul

Maybe the ones who drifted away

Will find themselves one day.

Lost

Go ahead, tell me what you are searching for,

The trees whisper, mimicking the sound of the ocean.

Whistling and breezing into her ear

She looks past every twinkle she sees

Discovers a mountain where her soul should be

Wonders where she places herself when everybody leaves

You have made me lose everything I hold close to me

I cannot see the blues and the greens in your version of reality.

Her mind is a spring day

The calming breeze of the trees swaying in unison with her thoughts

The sun streaming in through the open window blinding her from his flaws

She cannot find the letters she needs,

She cannot tell them what it is she seeks

She continues to lie there,

Simple sounds swaying into her

As she ignores her search for more.

A Time Forgot

She is an old soul

Staring at a painting

Of a time long forgot

Where the waves crashing onto the shore

Becomes the blood coursing through her veins.

Slowly she reaches out

Yearning for the bright ebony

Of the youth she has lost.

The ghost of a shadow flitters

Across the turquoise blanket

Shimmering into existence

To form an image.

But it's concealed, hard to make out

The darkness engulfs everything

And she is lost again.

She may appear in youth,

As she gazes into another world

But she is the matter of stardust

In the make-up of an old soul.

Conflicting Galaxies

I am just the stardust in your galaxy.

There is a yearning for me

to reach out

to grab onto the atoms of your being.

When will I learn

that the sun doesn't need the earth to survive?

And years and years pass by

with a turning of a soul in the branch of the universe,

one day I will try to be more

but my star can never be as big as your planet.

In the end aren't we searching for the same matter?

If Only

If only I could open you up

Read you like a book

Discover what thoughts lie inside

All the secrets you refuse to cry

You stand there with a vacant look

You hide your hurt with a smile

Your sorrow with empty tears.

I wonder if I read all your files

You'd be able to hide all your fears.

I want to love you

Spread myself over your insecurities

Take back every whisper I speak

Stop myself from hurting you.

Your sprinklings of okay

Are like droplets of snow that pretend to be rain

They falsify your words

And slowly they break your façade.

If only you were a book

Then surely I could just take a look

Flick over the yellowing pages

Reach the part that tells me what to do

Reach the part that tells me your truth.

Free-Falling

it's too much, their hearts overflowing,

over-spilling. A tidal wave rips across their heart

as they stare at each other. They can feel their insides tighten,

is that possible? Is that healthy?

They learned the meaning of the sun

when their souls touched for the first time

mixing into each other

keeping them awake

free-falling into the stardust, spinning away from reality

flying across the vast blue with wind piercing at their lungs

losing breath.

Emotions swim inside of her body

flowing through every vessel,

she is drowning when she looks at him

unprepared.

She forgot to bring her life jacket

because his eyes said she would drown,

what a pity she can't swim

when her soul meets his.

We are shouting "be brave!"

as she prepares to fly away

you see she cannot stay next to him and

let her galaxy fade away.

Such a shame she cannot see

that he only wants to help her float

he loves the beauty in her sea

he loves the stars that flow.

Now as she drifts away we start to sing a different chorus

one where lakes turn into rivers.

"He loves you!" We try and scream,

but her body has disappeared.

Still no harm has been done,

for the friendship they have fished for

remains in their soul

as they continue to fall in love.

Self Love Is A Crime

Inch by inch a nettle settles deep inside

Filling me up

Teasing my soul with each little rise

Into a body full of basic desires

Disguised by societies forgetful greed.

We are made to feel disgusted by a temple

Full of flowers and blossoms,

A temple created to spread only stardust and atoms

Discarded to make way for a world that thrives off our self-doubt.

To worship this temple is to worship a sin,

Misguided I continue to disagree

As my soul inches closer and closer to fulfilling my needs,

I disobey every superficial philosophy

With every touch I pour into me

And to every flowering goddess I ask only one thing

That you do the same and rise up, fulfil your own spring.

Love Yourself

I'm finding it hard to

      love me

I'm wondering if everyone else struggles with this same insecurity,

Looking at themselves and not knowing where they fit

It doesn't seem like it

Everyone I see shines bright, looks confident

I tell myself this is how they see me

But that's a lie; we all know my brain's a warped reality

Of finding it hard to love this skin I'm in when that skin is the same one blocking my

Confidence.

Body positivity never really became me

I discovered something new, something raw, something terrifying,

The fear of looking at a reflection wondering whose skin this is

Does everyone else suffer this same consequence?

I unlocked the secret to happiness

It was a big bronze key in the shape of a star

The door spoke to me and said

"If you can find the one thing in life

That reminds you who you are

That encourages you to follow your path

If you can find the entity that reminds you what you've seen

That shows you the sparkling dust of what you could've been

Then for the rest of this fleeting existence

Everything will come easy

Because you've found what you needed to breathe."

Oh but door, I replied

What if this thing rejects your whole, your outsides and insides

What if you reach and it stumbles backwards

How do you survive?

The door could not reply.

Missing You

Birds are drowning inside of me

I'm a cage that clips their wings

They can't flutter so I'll watch them sink

Pools of red and I can feel how deep.

They've mistaken my lungs for trees

And they're trying to make a nest out of paper leaves

If only you were here

You'd carve a door in my chest

Feel your way in and help them live

You'd fashion wings from our skin

Then they'd begin to fly and I'd learn to breathe

I'd make a home big enough for their next of kin

And you'd lie on a bed of flowers they sent us as a gift.

Not Everyone Gets To Live Forever

You have told me you want to live forever,

Exist in a universe where you will infinitely matter

And your presence will not disappear once

Your ashes have risen.

For you do not look forward to the end

And the idea that in generations to come

Your stories will cease to exist,

The name you sketch on paper

Becomes a forgotten memory in a child's mind

Always forgetting that you live in mine,

You exist in the words I write on memoirs

The thoughts that flow into my lyrics

You stay alive for eternity in the poetry I continue to write.

You see I can't get you out of all the things I do

Every word I spill onto paper has become about you,

So how can you possibly fade from this world

When you take up my universe in consistent swirls?

The Universe Has Bigger Plans

There is a place in my heart where you once lay

But do not mistake, I have not yet purged you out

Your essence still trickles into my dreams when I am drifting far off on another planet

Gravity askew, with my sense of direction lifted

No longer a clear path, just fragments and lessons

But I do not fear the unknown, even when it grapples my throat and twists its way like a winding snake

I have learnt to grow with the shifting hues and the rotating earth

I spin on an axis made up of forgotten hurt

There was a time when I thought this meant forever

But I am learning how to understand fate better

There is no ending in eternity

And destiny does not leave any of us in peace

We are subjects to the eternal shift

Like dying stars we are simply atoms that used to exist

I am fragments in a galaxy that is much larger than me

And although you exist in my memories

The space you occupy is no longer startling for there is no other universe I belong

You were never meant to be here for long and I am settling into a new rhythm

Gliding through time, revelling in my lack of resistance

There is a beauty in letting go of what is no longer serving.

A pebble in an ocean will question its worth

Amongst so many drops it loses its touch

Floating with no direction

Sweeping steadily upon a stream that carries it in waves

I wonder whether its direction has any purpose

This ink from my pen seeps onto the page

And leaves a mark that makes me question its depth

Just like a pebble losing its own sense

The stream of the ink swirling to form words

Paints on the page a black ocean of hurt

Just like a pebble ripples within the earth

I wonder if my voice is worth being heard.

I Trust You

To be me is scary

To show my scars as works of art leaves me feeling wary

I don't want my ego to take control

Let my trauma stop me from flowing with other souls

My past isn't an epitaph of how I'll grow

I know when the person I put on show

Isn't vulnerable enough

Doesn't open up

I know that's okay, I know you'll understand

But I don't want to be pretend, I want my hand to fit in your hand

I want to show my cracked vase

And I want you to see it as God's plan.

You see growing up I was always the weird kid

Came on too strong, didn't fit in

And the people who accepted me eventually left

Then I was left staring at a cracked mirror wondering what was next

But don't think I'm too weak because of my past

I know I shouldn't be too scared

Should learn to trust you're not here to rip me apart

Although I try to be approachable

It comes off as reproachable

Because when I was vulnerable it was met with a light made of gas

And my intelligence meant nothing, I was put down until I spoke crass

I'm sorry that while you stand there and open up

I reply with flowers disguised as thorns

Scared if I let you get close

Once again I'll be left alone.

Embracing Emotions

You ask me where this bottle goes

When I spill my emotions into it and watch it drift

                                    Out to sea

I hope as it swims further away from me

I can distance myself from every way in which it plagues my being

I don't want to scare you with these secrets

Don't want my emotions to be the reason

You can't stand to be near me,

You say you're okay,

I pray I find a way to be less of myself.

                             But you don't get to drink out of the bottle

It's mine to keep and its message tells me I am enough

These emotions might scare you

But they're mine to keep

I can no longer silence a demon that wants to sing

It yells with black swirling in its pit

Because it feels and it's not scared to exist

The bottle doesn't get very far before it begins to drift back

Curl up on the sand, lay there and you'll find what I lack

I am lying on the bobbing waves drifting closer to the horizon

The bottle has spilled open now and I don't care what feelings are staring to ripen.

Flaws

We are beings of imperfect flaws

And yes I know you've all said this before

That our image is tied to our self-worth

For it is a difficulty

To admit we suffer jealousy, animosity

That we are humans with a sense of depravity

And gentle words cascading out of their mouths

Telling us stories of our beauty is something we must doubt

To accept that we have a shadow is a harder thing to do

Because to accept vices means opening up to truth

And resisting the demon inside of us that looms

The one that tell us we're stones that cut

Not soft pebbles on oceans each their own kind of love

But competition to be the last one who rusts

And even now I struggle to admit my vices

Because they show I'm a person who suffers their own crisis.

Labelled As Thinking

The rains fogging up my glasses

Clouding up my senses

I can't see where I begin and my thoughts end

I name them as they come

But they get harder to let go of

Some days I hold on longer even though I know it's not good for me

It's my own kind of twisted therapy

Reflecting on warped memories

Keeping them locked in a box in my head

Maybe if I disguise them as poor decisions

They'll find a place that isn't warped by egotism

I'm trying to wipe my glasses so I can see

Taking a breath doesn't come easy

For a second the sky clears

And my mind becomes the silence in between.

Looking After Myself

I can't explain what it feels like to embrace pain

The satisfaction that crying brings when tears spill out of me and wash me away

Now I sit here in mourning and I long for a way to nourish my inner child

Envelop her in a tight embrace and tell her everything is okay

I have seen her deteriorate with every passing day

She tried to cling onto gratitude but all she could feel was pain

Hate and animosity towards self was all she knew until it seeped into the ones who tried to love her too

How can I reach in time to that parallel world where she clings on and let her know it's okay to let go

That loving yourself is not a mirror of being consumed by ego

But simply a way to embrace the essence of her entire beautiful existence.

Why couldn't the ones in her life show her what love was?

She was trying to seek it from mates who hadn't discovered their own soul

As if sinking tightly into them would help her gain growth.

What can I tell her about death?

About how dying is not the end but a continuation of her ever-glowing love.

What should she do when she is all alone?

I pray for her growth

I am her parent, her carer and I want to stomp on those who sought nothing but chaos

Tried to stifle her, diminish her glittery pearls into something worthless

Even when they loved her it was never enough because she projected fear onto them

Even her soul mate looked at her and called her a burden like that was her make up

Like the burden was who she was rather than his own trauma

What a tragedy to be left alone with only your self-loathing as company

My rainbow child, I want you to recognise your beauty

I want to hold you while you cry into me

Let me be your nurturer, your friend, your lover

Let me shower you with all the reasons you're a wonder

One day you will look in the mirror and see stars looking back at you

One day I bathe under this moonlight and I pray for your truth.

A New Energy

A deep breath in. A deep breath out.

The leaves rustle as the earth sighs,

exhaling out a long breath

held in for so long that the lungs of the trees felt tight

now the grass flickers as the leaves spin onto the ground

and every whistle of wind is the earth calling out love letters disguised in sounds

petals dance, their arms sprouting with life

as the clouds twirl around in the sky

even the waves of the ocean let the oxygen out and in

as mother earth whispers her songs within the wind.

Change Comes To Me Like Spring

I feel the need to write

Put down my thoughts into a form that doesn't feel like a plight

Of difficulty, of trying to figure out a place in this room

I know I don't belong here

I am a sprinkle of atoms next to a different universe

I feel myself drifting amongst lost souls

Trying to find my way home

And I wonder why I keep losing my grip

On the things I held dear

They soared so far away if I reach out I'll lose myself, gain a sense of fear

I want to be brave and tell myself to hold on tighter

To the things that keep me going, the people

Who understand what it means to be a fighter

I am tired of fitting in now

I tried to block the child inside of me for the people who didn't care

And she was suffering alone wishing for my hand

I blocked her away, told myself I'm better off finding my own space

But my inner child just wants a place to be free, be herself

And I just want to be me

A lone lily drifting on a riverbed

Losing petals but gaining strength

I feel myself bloom open now

Spring is around the corner and I've gained a structure

Winter's cold seeps into me one last time

I feel the changes and I am learning what it means to live on a lifeline

No longer trying to swim next to the others

Learning to drift with the wind

Stop and shudder

Close my eyes

Feel something deeper.

Life

and then one day I stopped overlooking it all,

I heard the birds in the tree sing a song of territory

I listened to the way people talked to each other

the way the mum on the bus smiled at her child like he put the sun in the sky

the way that group of friends laughed too loudly

or the sound of the footsteps from someone overtaking me,

I saw the sky for the first time

and I touched the trees and felt them pulsating beneath me

so alive and so free

and I fell in love with strangers, I fell in love with my surroundings,

I fell in love with that girl humming along to her music

and that boy reading that over-turned 500 page book,

and I felt the breeze of the world's life brush through me

and I didn't know I could feel so alive.

Meet My Friend: Death

I have seen death all my life

Crossed paths with him

He always seems to be laughing

But he scares me.

I don't know how to talk to him

He is an unknown entity

A figure I don't actually see

And I have run from him

But some moments were harder than others

Then I was spending time with death

Wondering what secrets he kept

And we conversed like old friends meeting in secret.

That's a memory I will always live with

I'll keep it deep under my skin

Underneath the flakes and cracks and I won't let him in.

But then I felt wind rushing over my face today

My body was flowing up and down

Sometimes I lost control, bent backwards and felt the sky caressing my throat

But I never let go

As I was staring at the sky

I realised how quickly time passes by

My heart swelled and tears brimmed in my eyes

It's been a while since I cried

And then I felt that soft breath on my hair and I remembered that I am here

Now death is watching me even as I write this

He smiles from somewhere I can't see

I am aware he's getting closer but I don't want to believe

Maybe I am naive in thinking that I am different, unique

But eventually death gets what he seeks

No one is above him and he creates meaning

Because this is the last time I will feel this in my feet

When the ground is something I can't reach

Nothing is pulling me down I'm grasping what I lost

Coming back to me, understanding what makes me happy.

Death can laugh all he wants

I can't hear him

Over the wind.

Peace

I feel peace

Or is this serenity?

I'm not sure, my whole life I spent searching for clarity

Only to find myself warped by my own skin

I'm here now

Allah has taught me to surrender

I can't feel anything else

At my worst I feel my best

I don't know who to thank

But my soul feels light and I owe it to every place

I stepped in

Seeing each person feel

Feel so deeply helped me reach new worlds

Broken hurt turned into something else

My friends patched up my broken wings

The loved sent me help through words they sing

I know now

Peace is within my reach.

Metamorphosis

These changes within me

Flow through every part of my being

Like the wide open sea

I'm beginning to float with the tide

Learn how to be alive

And I can sense there is a metamorphosis

That with each breath these memories are making spaces in places
I didn't realise exists

I look behind and I see the souls left behind

Look around and find myself staring at the ground

It's only my reflection now

But then the sky soars down

Envelops me in blues, purples and pinks

Secrets disguised in the wind of what my future will bring.

I'm not listening

Right now I'm focusing on the sounds

The cold pricking my hands as I write

The whispers of my bones

And the wind on my soul.

Printed in Great Britain
by Amazon

22168524R00067